Trust in Yourself

Library of Congress Catalog Card Number: 97-10700
ISBN: 0-88396-450-3

Manufactured in the United States of America
First Printing: April, 1997

♻ This book is printed on recycled paper.

Library of Congress Cataloging-in-Publication Data

Fargo, Donna.
    Trust in yourself : thoughts about listening to your heart and
  becoming the person you want to be / Donna Fargo.
        p.   cm.
    ISBN 0-88396-450-3 (alk. paper)
    1. Self-realization — Poetry. I. Title.
  PS3556.A7145T78   1997
  811'.54 — DC21   97-10700
                                                          CIP

Trust in Yourself

Thoughts About Listening to Your Heart
and Becoming the Person You Want to Be

Donna Fargo

Blue Mountain Press®

P.O. Box 4549, Boulder, Colorado 80306

Introduction

This book is about not giving up when the going gets tough. It's about finding strength when it looks like all hope is gone. It's about having faith that there are answers inside us to the questions and the doubts and the fears that keep confronting us. It's about talking to the mountain we're trying to move and believing in our hearts that we can move it.

If you believe as I do that the heart is worthy of our trust, I encourage you to trust in yourself, and I dedicate this book to those of you who encourage others to trust in themselves.

Donna Fargo

Trust in Yourself

I believe all of us have
a built-in compass to help
us get to wherever we desire to go.
Don't forget to trust that compass,
and refer to it often,
for with that trusting
will come the strength to bear
whatever life deals you.

Don't get led astray. Ask your heart for the truth, and it will come up with the answer and the good judgment to make the decisions you'll need to make. Love everyone, and don't question love's reception. Do the best you can. Live each day as it comes. We can't get ahead of ourselves anyway.

Remember: just as you have questions now, somewhere inside you, and down the road, there will be better answers and workable solutions. It takes patience and trust to get through life's changes when you're trying to reach goals, solve problems, and make dreams come true. Though at times it may seem more than you can take, I know you are strong, and you can handle whatever comes your way. Trust in yourself.

I Know You're Going Through Some Changes Now, and I'd Make Life Easier for You If I Could

I'd answer all those questions you have,
try to help you settle your confusion about
what to do now and in the future.
I'd heal your hurts and fix your problems
with an eternal bond of love,
so you would never come "unglued."
I just wanted you to know that
I'd make it easier for you if I could.

I'd find you a way over every obstacle,
an answer to every prayer, a peaceful resolution
to every challenge and conflict that causes
the kind of hurt I know you must be feeling.
I don't want to meddle or impose,
but if you need to talk, I will listen,
and I'll do what I can.
I just wanted you to know that
I'd make it easier for you if I could.

None of us is promised any easy magic solutions,
and often it seems we must find our way alone
through our brokenness.
It seems everyone has some kind of "cross to bear,"
and often the weight of it cannot be shared.
But I just wanted you to know that
I wish I could help you dry your tears, and
I'd make life easier for you if I could.

Just know that I'm thinking of you,
praying for you, and trusting with you
that all the things you're going through
will work together for a mutual good, and
you will finally see reasons for all that's
happened, if that's what you need.
Eventually and surely, there will be
light where there was darkness.
Don't despair. It will get better.
I know you're going through some changes now,
and I'd make life easier for you if I could.

I Hope You Know...

I want to be a source of comfort to you
   ... like a blanket to wrap around you when you're cold
   ... like a pillow for you to use to rest your head
   ... like arms to hold you when you're weary and feeling alone
   ... like a handkerchief to catch your tears

I want to be a source of strength to you
   ... like sunshine when you need warmth in your life
   ... like music that soothes your emptiness and fills a lonely space
   ... like a meal when you're hungry and want to eat
   ... like a shoulder you can lean on for support

I want to be a source of love to you
  ... like someone who offers praise and never
     pressure
  ... like someone who is there to talk to when
     you need to talk
  ... like someone who is there for you to be
     whatever it is you need
  ... like someone who loves you just the way
     you are

I want to be a source of certainty for you
that you always have someone on your side
  ... to give you hope that there is a way
     through everything
  ... to give you confidence that there is a light
     at the end of the tunnel
  ... to be a voice that says, "Congratulations!
     You've made it through another one!"
  ... to share with you every challenge, every
     joy, every trial in your life.

Sometimes You Just Have to Carry On

*W*hen life hands you a surprise and you wind up somewhere you didn't plan on being, maybe it's time to stop and rest, read some good books, regroup, and stop trying so hard. Do some things you may not have taken the time to do for yourself before. Take time to study; all of us need to be constantly growing in wisdom. Feed your soul by being quiet, by just being rather than doing.

Try not to worry or fuss or fume. Try to look at this situation as a challenge rather than an obstacle, a time to develop patience. Say to yourself: "I can handle this. This is not too big for me." Realize you can change your attitude even if you can't change the circumstances.

Look closely at your troubles. Don't let them cause you to give up. Befriend them. Say: "I'm not afraid. I'm going to learn from you." Feel them lose their power over you. Allow them to teach you some lesson you needed to learn and move on.

You're going to deal with this. You're going to uncover some things about yourself even you didn't know. You're going to find strength you didn't know you had and grace to handle whatever comes along.

Just remember that everything changes, so it's just a matter of time until this trial will be over and you will draw strength from the knowledge that even though life handed you a challenge, you survived; you carried on.

There's a Light at the End of This Tunnel, and You Will Make It Through

I can't remove the worry from your consciousness. *I can't remove the dread of having to face another challenge. I can't carry your burden for you. I can't even help you carry it. But I know you are concerned, as you should be, and I wanted you to know that I'm thinking of you especially during this time.*

I also want you to know that I'm praying for you and sending you good thoughts. I know that you are strong, that you can handle this, and soon you'll be on the other side, and you'll be fine. I know you're doing all that you know to do, and I just wanted you to know that I care about you. There's a light at the end of this tunnel, and you will make it through.

10 *Things to Remember When Your Feelings Have Been Trampled On*

1. Whether family members, people at work, or best friends have hurt you badly, put yourself in their shoes and treat them the way you would want to be treated, even if you think they don't deserve it.

2. If you've heard something you didn't want to hear, remember it may not be 100% true. So lighten up. If it's not urgent, put off thinking about it for a couple of days. Forgive the person who may have wronged you; don't forget, you're doing this for yourself, too. Prove to yourself that you can practice what you believe. Try to be as understanding of others as you would want them to be of you.

3. Even if you lose a battle, that doesn't mean you've lost the "war." Act according to how you want to feel about yourself. Don't judge what others do if you don't want them to judge you.

4. Remember, what other people do is their responsibility. Don't let them cause you to carry a grudge and let their actions weigh you down. They are not responsible for your actions, no matter what they do. You are.

5. If people have said something untrue about you or done something intentionally to hurt you, wish good things for them — even if you don't feel like it. Ask for them what you desire for yourself, and it will draw those things to you.

6. *If you've made a mistake or disappointed yourself or others, apologize quickly and earnestly. Let your remorse teach you how to have compassion for others when they make mistakes. Nobody's perfect, even though we all try to be. If someone can't accept your apology, that's okay, too. Just do the right thing and go on.*

7. *Listen objectively and talk mindfully. Don't take things so personally. If you have the right attitude, no one can really hurt you. If you need to vent your anger, go outside and throw rocks on the cement, take a walk, or, better yet, sing... it will help put the melody back in your life. It's hard to be angry while you're singing.*

8. *If you think people are making fun of you or someone you love, disarm them, not with your fist, but with your best smile. Give them something they don't know how to give. Speak to them; be bold. Ask that they be blessed and you'll be blessed, too. Forgiveness is a powerful thing; it will help your body and soul. Don't let others cause you to act the way they've acted toward you, and remember that they have a right to do whatever they choose also.*

9. *Don't hide your hurts and pains and feelings inside where they can harden your heart. Use common sense and understanding to process them. Don't react just from your feelings; respond with maturity rather than childish habit. You won't regret it.*

10. *Get in touch with the person you want to be and become that. Listen to your heart... you can find the answer there to every question you have. Remember, no matter how you're treated, just treat others the way you would want to be treated when your feelings are getting trampled on.*

Look Inside Your Own Heart
for the Answers That You Need

If you have a problem and you don't know what to do, sometimes it's a good idea to advise yourself as though you're giving advice to someone else. After all, you know yourself better than anyone.

Think back on other problems you've solved and the steps you took to reach your goal, and apply those principles to this one. If you've tried to solve this same problem before and failed, try a different approach. Take small steps and stop thinking you can do it all at once; some results can only be achieved over time. If you're trying to break a deeply ingrained habit, keep reminders close by for quick reference to stay focused on the new habit you're trying to make. Think of the new behavior in terms of a reward rather than a sacrifice. Just a slight shift in your attitude can alleviate frustration and stress.

Resolve to be your own best example for whatever it is you're trying to do. Integrity is a very personal quality; be honest with yourself. Have a philosophy and live by it. Ask yourself what you believe and act as though you believe it. Beliefs are wasted if not acted upon. Ask yourself what kind of person you want to be and become it. When you make mistakes, start over. Honor your nature and your uniqueness, but also recognize that you can change things you don't like about yourself if they don't serve the person you know you're capable of becoming. When in doubt, ask your heart the question, and trust it to come up with the answer.

Think of Today
as a New Beginning

Although your life may not be as perfect as you'd like, you can always look around and find people who are worse off than you. Be grateful for the problems you <u>don't</u> have. Take some quiet time away from the noise and haste, and count your blessings. Take inventory. Start with the people in your life who bring you joy and satisfaction; they are a gift to you.

Be thankful for the choices you've made, both good and bad. Accept your mistakes and go on. You can't change them anyway. Learn from them and apply what you've learned. Don't allow them to have more influence on your life than they deserve. They're just mistakes; they're not your final grade. Besides, making them now may keep you from making bigger mistakes in life later. Use them to help you with other choices so you won't keep doing the same things again.

Go outside and touch the sky. Enjoy the colors of the landscape; romp and play on the grassy ground. Smile at the world, and marvel at the wonders of the universe. Embrace the air; be thankful. Don't allow any negative feelings to creep into your consciousness. Feel the power of your own acceptance. Put a positive spin on every thought you have.

Bask in the glory of awareness. Experience the joy of praise. You're alive! Appreciate the gift of your life.

Believe in Yourself
and Be Patient...

Your Life Is a Masterpiece Unfolding

Although you may not feel that you're making progress because certain things you want to happen in your life haven't happened yet, this place you are in now is important, too. Waiting for your efforts to produce results may test your patience and resolve, but I'm impressed with your control and perseverance as you take each small step toward your dreams and goals.

Even though you may not be able to see it now, I just wanted to tell you that you are a tapestry in progress, a masterpiece unfolding. You are worthy. You are deserving. You are loved... even when it doesn't feel like it. Believe it and be patient. Your dreams will happen, and someday you will look back on this moment in time and understand the meaning of this place you are in now, as it, too, adds depth, dimension, and form to the work of art... that is you.

You Can Do Anything
You Believe You Can

If there's a goal you want to reach, resolve to start doing something about it. Stop procrastinating. Write out what you want to do and how you plan to do it. It's the same as if you were planning a trip: you get a map, make your preparations, and then start traveling the right road.

Do something every day to move the roadblocks that stand in your way. Keep it simple. Trust your instincts. Do one thing at a time. Remember... if you haven't reached your goal and you keep doing the same things you're doing now, you'll keep ending up in similar places to where you are now.

Once you start making progress, you will be magically propelled toward eventual reward. Just keep listening and taking direction from inside you. Every effort you make tells your being that you're serious. Action empowers us toward more action. Be patient; your dreams will not come true overnight. But start now, and go with love and courage and confidence. Don't be afraid. You can do anything you believe you can.

You're This Kind of Beautiful

You have the kind of qualities and characteristics that make people around you glad you're in their world. You have the kind of character that reaches out to others to make the world a better and more beautiful place in which to live. Your beauty is not consumed with its own needs and prejudices but finds satisfaction in giving hope and acceptance and approval to others. It is an internal, soothing kind of beauty that activates the love and appreciation mechanisms in other people, making it easier for everyone to live together. You're this kind of beautiful.

You're the kind of beautiful that doesn't change with the weather or a crisis in life. It is a kind of beauty that provides light in the world for others to use to guide themselves out of difficult circumstances. Although its glow may dim at times when presented with a new challenge, yours is the kind of beauty that will survive the hard places in life, allowing you to learn from them. It will sustain you. You have this kind of beauty.

This kind of beautiful comes from the heart and is powered by a love for others, a desire to be good, to do good, to help and not hurt anyone. It's easy for someone to enhance their appearance on the outside, but to be beautiful inside means reaching out to others with kindness and thoughtfulness and generosity. It is wanting the best for everyone, not just for yourself. It has to do with compassion. That's the way you are. That's the kind of beauty you have.

Being this kind of beautiful allows you to identify with other people's shortcomings in life. This kind of beautiful knows that you must be able to love, forgive, and accept others, or your beauty will lose its essence and its gift, which is the desire to love.

This kind of beauty is soft and easy to be around. It gives more than it takes. It doesn't judge others harshly. It's not egotistical or proud. It doesn't try to change others. It accepts. It shows itself with open arms, not clenched fists; with smiles, not frowns; with joy and laughter, not negativity and reprimands. Being this kind of beautiful is contagious; it lifts others up to accept themselves and to experience their own gift of beauty. Being this kind of beautiful makes others glad to be alive and to know you. You're this kind of beautiful. Thank you for your wonderful example.

I Just Know
You're Going to Be Fine

When things are not right in your life,
    they're not right in mine.
So whatever you're feeling, I'm feeling it, too;
    I know you're going to be fine.

I'll hold you up like you've held me before;
    wherever you are is where I'll be.
This will give me a chance to be strong for you,
    like you have been strong for me.

No matter what you're going through,
    you can count on me all the way.
Ask me anything, and I'll do it for you...
    I'll listen. I'll care. I'll pray.

You're not alone, so don't be afraid.
Two heads are better than one.
We'll get through this together with flying colors
before it is over and done.

Just take it easy; rest for a change.
Tell me what to do. You know the ropes.
When it seems like your world is falling apart,
lean on me; I'll carry your hopes.

Whether you're in a valley or on a mountaintop,
if there are troubles in your world or mine,
I'll be here for you like you've been for me;
I just know you're going to be fine.

I Still Believe There's Hope

I've been in places where I felt I had no choice in the matter. I've cried because I had no clue about how to help myself. But I've always believed that we must make the best of whatever life hands us and that no one can expect more of us than the best that we can do.

I know the need to change sometimes feels urgent, and though I'd gladly try to help you if I could, no one can move this mountain for you. The answers you need are inside you, just like the answers I need are inside me. They may not come easily and they may seem to be hiding, but I encourage you to trust yourself enough to follow your own heart and intuition; it's really the only way to go.

Doing what <u>you</u> believe, not depending so much on others but asking yourself for the answers to your own personal questions, may be what will keep you going until you reach your goal.

I don't know about you, but I refuse to stop trying to make my life better, and if I think I can make a difference by changing something that I do, I won't give up until I do. I would rather go down fighting and hoping and trying than giving up or acquiescing, wouldn't you?

In the meantime, I'll pray for you and you pray for me. No matter what the trial, no matter what others say, let's hold on to each other and steadfastly believe that we will not be defeated. There just have to be some answers someday. I still believe there's hope.

If There's a Dream in Your Heart... Go for It!

If you're treading new ground
or fighting the same old battle,
    don't give up.
Continue to dream, plan, and do.
Try something different if you're stuck.
Do whatever your heart tells you.
Give yourself credit for all you've
    accomplished.
Most dreams that come true are born
    out of desire
and fueled by preparation and action.
Don't be afraid. You can do it.
I know you can.

Dare to Reach Higher

A *winner is just someone who*
*   never stops trying*
One who succeeds is just a fighter
*   who won't stay down*
A spiritual giant is just another
*   natural man:*
*   a spirit, mind, and body*
Who believed and acted on the truths
*   until he reached the higher ground*

Faith is made stronger
*   only by exercising it*
By believing... together...
*   with the Spirit...*
*   against the natural tide*
Knowledge is faith acted upon
*   time and time again*
And love paves the way
*   for the dreamer who has tried*

So dare to reach higher than
*   you've ever reached before*
Your dream is not impossible
*   if only you can believe*
Be good... be faithful...
*   prepare... and trust...*
Then rest and rejoice...
*   and you will receive.*

Hope Is Just Around the Corner

If fear is faith turned upside down
*   and hate is love wrong side out*
If sad is happy in reverse
*   and a blessing is the opposite of a curse...*

If apathy was once care that has died
*   and success is failure's other side*
If dark is the bottom side of light
*   and day is the morning side of night...*

Maybe we should not despair
*   when the news seems always bad*
If hope is just around the corner
*   on the other side of sad*

To find the answers that we need
*   maybe struggle is the place to start*
To solve the great mysteries of life
*   it seems we should consult the heart.*

Love Knows No Door

In the sweet by and by
    You will understand why
And when your wings are strong again
    I know you'll fly
Though your faith has been shaken
    Keep trying your best
And cling to one truth
    Above all the rest

Whatever the question
    love is the answer
It works no matter
    how you feel
For love knows no door
    that it cannot open
And no broken heart
    that it cannot heal

I'll Still Believe in You

When you're at the end of the road
   and you have to turn around
When you're hanging on by a thread and
   you need someone to ease you to the ground
When you've got no more magic up your sleeve
   and you want someone to talk about things to
I hope you know that I'll be here
   and I'll still believe in you

When things are going great for you
   I'll be there by your side
To cheer you on and say... "You did it!
   Now just enjoy the ride."
When you're stuck between the triumphs
   and don't know what else to do
I hope you know that I'll be here
   and I'll still believe in you

When you doubt your own ability
 to face another mountain
When you're thirsty for some water
 but you can't get to the fountain
No matter what the challenge
 no matter how well you do or don't do
I hope you know that I'll be here
 and I'll still believe in you

If you just need a sounding board
 I will do the best I can
To listen, accept, advise if you want
 I'll try to understand
Whatever your heart desires
 no matter what you're going through
I know you know, but I'll say it again...
 I'll still believe in you

Of Course You Can!

When you want to do something and you hear your own voice telling you that there's no use trying... When it's saying to you "What makes you think you can do this?"

Remember there's another voice you can listen to... the voice of hope and encouragement. It's not the one that says "You can't do this." It's the one that says... "Of course you can!"

Many people lack the confidence, self-esteem, and will to try to succeed. Some people are good starters but not good finishers. Some may be afraid they'll lose; some may even be afraid they'll win. Some become discouraged because they listen to the voice that talks them out of trying and into giving up. They hear "You might as well forget it; you'll never do this."

But there's another message that you can also hear if you will only listen. It's the one that says... "Of course you can!"

Like the flower created from a single seed will eventually bloom, the dream inside us all has the potential to come true. Where there's a will, there's a won't, but there's also a way. Just remember: people choose also by not choosing. It's not just what we do, but sometimes it's what we don't.

So plan it, work at what you want, and don't be afraid to dream. Think of all those times that you've reached your goals before. Ignore the voices that want to discourage you; you don't have to entertain them. It's always up to you to listen, not to the voice that says you can't, but to the one that says... "Of course you can!"

My Wishes for You...

I *wish you love and happiness*
Perfect health your whole life through
As much money as you need
    to make life easier
To do the things you want to

I wish you joy and satisfaction
The appreciation you so deserve
Courage when you're fearful
When you're about to lose your nerve

I wish you good friends to call on
A playful heart to keep you young
Special memories to hold on to
Pretty melodies to be sung

I hope you have someone to talk to
And to be with when you please
To share life's special things with
Like a walk among the trees

To share a blanket in the wintertime
To protect you from the cold
To picnic with in the summertime
To hug and kiss and hold

Remember, things don't always work out
*   for the best in life*
But you can make the best of everything
Just turn those lessons from your journey
Into songs that you can sing

If I could package up all my wishes for you
With a ribbon and a bow
Whatever you want would be yours for the asking
Whatever you need, wherever you go.

You're So Important to Me

There are some people in my life who really make a difference. They mean so much that I wonder how I could ever get along without them. When I look back, I can see the void that they filled in my heart. That's the way I feel about you.

You can brighten up a room just by walking in. Talking to you on the phone makes my day. You're considerate. You don't say you'll be somewhere and then not show up. You're as good as your word. You're thoughtful and you're genuine, and you give others the benefit of the doubt. You go forward with confidence yet keep pride in its place.

You make me feel special because you often go out of your way for me. Your loyalty is a treasure, and I enjoy being around you. You mean what you say and you say what you mean. You're not afraid to work, to do more than your part, to learn something new, to grow, to fail, to succeed, to take chances, to risk, to dream, to say you're wrong, to forgive, to go all out for someone if you believe it's right. I love these things about you; they set you apart from others. You're different, you're rare, and I hope these qualities in you never change.

In case you don't know it by now, you're so important to me. I appreciate you, and I feel blessed to have you in my life.

I'll Be There for You

I will go with you through
whatever you're going through
if you want me to.

If you're down and out,
I'll be there for you.
If you're on top of the world,
I'll celebrate with you.

I'll try to ease your pain
when you're hurting;
I'll listen if you need to talk.
I'll pray for you and bear
your burdens with you.

I'll cry with you
and laugh with you.
I'll be loyal to you.

I'll wish the best for you.
I'll be there for you forever,
or for as long
as you want me.

Hang Tough!

We all get discouraged and want to quit sometimes. It's a part of life.

But we know, too, not to take it all so seriously, that this too, no matter how serious it feels, will pass and change into another lesson on life's pathway, another memory of some place in life's journey.

Just remember that you are loved.
You are beautiful.
You are rare and special, and
I will always believe in you.

About the Author

Photo by Yervand Mikailian

Donna Fargo is perhaps best known as "The Happiest Girl in the Whole U.S.A.," referring to the song she wrote and recorded in 1972, which won Donna numerous awards, including a platinum album and a Grammy for best country vocal performance. Her self-penned follow-up hit, "Funny Face," went platinum, too, and established Donna as the first female artist in country music history to have back-to-back million-selling number-one singles. Both songs also earned her gold records in Canada, Australia, and New Zealand.

Donna's other hit records include: "That Was Yesterday," "Somebody Special," "Superman," "You Were Always There," "You Can't Be a Beacon," "Don't Be Angry," "Do I Love You," and "U.S. of A.," to name just a few. She has received six Academy of Country Music awards, five Billboard awards, fifteen Broadcast Music Incorporated (BMI) writing awards, and two National Association of Recording Merchandisers awards for bestselling artist. She has been honored by the Country Music Association, the National Academy of Recording Arts and Sciences, and the Music Operators of America. As a writer, her most coveted awards, in addition to the Robert J. Burton Award that she won for "Most Performed Song Of The Year," are her Million-Airs Awards, presented to writers for attaining the blockbuster status of 1,000,000 or more performances.

Prior to achieving superstardom and becoming one of the most prolific songwriters in Nashville, Donna was an English teacher. It is her love of the English language and her desire to communicate sincere and honest emotions that compelled Donna to try her hand at writing something other than song lyrics. With these new writings, Donna hopes to tap that "sensitive place from where feelings come, as they are born and sculptured in the private confines of the heart." Anyone who has bought Donna's records and sung along with her songs will be delighted with this new avenue she has chosen for her talents. Anyone not so familiar with Donna's previous work will be both touched and inspired by her words.

Today, in addition to writing nonstop, Donna continues to tour, performing before sold-out capacity crowds.